Pisa in One Day

Enrico Massetti

Pisa in One Day

Enrico Massetti

Published by Enrico Massetti

ISBN: 978-1514735770

Pisa

Cathedral and Leaning Tower

Pisa is another ancient city, first Greek, then Etruscan and Roman; a great Maritime Republic and finally part of the Medici Grand Duchy of Tuscany.

Pisa developed its own architectural style by blending classical and oriental forms. Great Italian Gothic sculpture was also born at Pisa with Nicola Pisano's school which produced Giovanni Pisano, Arnolfo da Cambia, and Andrea and Nino Pisano.

From the early 11th to the late 14th centuries Pisa was one of the greatest and most active Italian centers of art. Proof of this is the remarkable group of buildings constituted by the Cathedral, the Baptistery, the Leaning Tower and the adjacent Cemetery which, in their unspoiled isolation, form one of the most solemn and enchanting corners in all of Italy.

We cannot even attempt to list the works of art produced by this extraordinary flowering in Pisa: from the superb bronze Doors by Bonanno (late 12th century) to the Pulpit by Giovanni Pisano (1310) in the Cathedral; from the mosaics, to the paintings by Cimabue, Andrea del Santo, Beccafumi, and Sodoma; from the inlaid woodwork in the choir, to the Tomb which Tino da Camaino sculptured for the Emperor Henry VII, and to the incredible collection of Greek, Roman and medieval sculptures which throng the four sides of the 14th-15th century Cemetery beneath a veritable treasure-house of medieval frescoes. The chain of artistic miracles continues unbroken in architectural setting untouched by the passing of the centuries.

The Leaning Tower

During its period of greatest prestige and power, Pisa, which was a rapidly expanding city, wanted to erect its most important church, crowned by what is now known as the Leaning Tower, the Baptistery and the Camposanto.

The architecture of the four structures, their harmony, wasn't the fruit of a single mind. In fact, the square is the result of the work of more than one brilliant architect working over several periods on the overall structure. Reinterpreting the geometry of architecture and borrowing from Islamic art, they invented a new style Romanesque.

Pre-dating the Florentine Renaissance this style is found in figurative art as well as in the work of exceptional artists such as Nicola and his son Giovanni, who influenced artists such as Brunelleschi, Donatello and Michelangelo himself.

The Baptistery

The Baptistery

Construction of the Pisa Baptistery was begun in 1153 by Diotisalvi, the architect who designed the church of Santo Sepolcro. The monument was rebuilt in 1278, as revealed in an inscription located between two pillars inside. There are no clear ideas regarding how work on the Baptistery proceeded.

The order of arches that encircle the Baptistery is decorated by heads and sculptures attributed to Nicola and Giovanni Pisano which are considered among the most important works.

At the center of the monument there is the beautiful baptismal font and, near the altar, the pulpit, work of the great Nicola Pisano in 1260.

The Camposanto

Cathedral from the Camposanto

The Pisa Camposanto (cemetery) was founded in 1277 following the design of Giovanni Simone, and it was completed in 1464. It was home to the marvelous series of frescoes which, beginning with The Triumph of Death, attributed to Buonamico Buffalmacco, and continuing with the works of Spinello Aretino, Antonio Veneziano, Andrea da Firenze, Taddeo Gaddi, Piero di Puccio and Benozzo Gozzoli, were disastrously ruined in the WWII bombing of August 1944.

Restoration of the frescoes proved to be difficult, and it was the work of "strappo", the act of detaching a fresco from a wall in order to transfer it to a canvas or other support, which revealed the original design of the works of the above mentioned artists. Restored to their original beauty, the sinopias are the main attraction of the *Museo delle Sinopie*.

The Duomo

The Duomo

An open space away from the ancient walls was chosen as a suitable place for the city's Duomo. After the victorious expedition of Palermo (1063), construction began under the direction of Buschetto.

In its conception, the Duomo, dedicated to Santa Maria Assunta, was intended to reflect the architectural style of the whole of the sacred structures around the dome.

However, 100 years later, another great architect, Rainaldo, conceived and directed the prolongation of the three bays, terminating the splendid facade and raising the nave to the completion of the Duomo, unique and grandiose, that we see today.

The Bell Tower known as The Leaning Tower

The Leaning Tower

The first stone of the Leaning Tower was laid on Assumption Day, 9 August 1173. While it is possible to locate the names of the artists who signed their works in the other buildings in the square, the Leaning Tower has no such autograph. This curious fact adds to the several hundred year of long debate over the first author and the first ten years of the construction of the Leaning Tower.

In the year 1185 the first signs of sagging foundations were seen, and the consequent inclination of the tower caused the halting of the construction for nearly a century. The continuation of the tower was entrusted to Giovanni di Simone who had been working on the bell tower of San Francesco.

The architect showed extraordinary skill in limiting the consequences of the inclination, thereby allowing construction to continue until 1284, the date of the defeat of the Meloria.

The final story of the bell tower, the seventh, used as a belfry. was conceived and realized by Tommaso Pisano approximately halfway through the 14th century.

San Paolo a Ripa d'Arno

San Paolo a Ripa d'Arno

Having finished our visit to the Cathedral of Pisa and the surrounding buildings, down Via S. Maria to the River Arno, we find the church of San Nicola and next, to in the 16th century Palazzo Reale (Royal Palace), overlooking the river: and before reaching the Citadel, we cross Ponte Solferino and walk down the other side of the river, coming to San Paolo a Ripa d'Arno, with a Romanesque facade similar to that of the Cathedral and containing excellent works of sculpture. Returning walking along the river and passing the bridge, we come to the extremely charming little church of S. Maria della Spina a jewel of Pisan-Gothic architecture.

Following the river to Ponte di Mezzo, past a row of beautiful old palaces, and passing the 17th century Loggia Banchi, we reach, by way of Via San Martino, in what was the quarter of the Arab merchants, the very ancient octagonal church of the Holy

Sepulcher (Santo Sepolcro) (12th century), with its picturesque interior. Here stands the great church of San Martino, containing several beautiful paintings.

National Museum of Pisa

National Museum of Pisa

Crossing the Ponte alla Fortezza, which affords magnificent views of the Lungarni (river banks), we come to the Lungarno Mediceo, where we find the National Museum of Pisa, an extremely important collection of paintings (Simone Martini, Fra Angelico, Masaccio, Gentile da Fin briano, Sodoma, etc., as well as a superb group of primitives) and of Greek, Roman, medieval and Renaissance sculpture.

Taking Via Giovanni di Simone, we come to the church of San Francesco (inside, frescoes by Taddeo Gaddi and Nicolo and Pietro Gerini), and from there to S. Catering, Gothic, with panel paintings by Traini and sculpture by Nina Pisano.

Palazzo della Carovana

Palazzo della Carovana

Going next to the Palazzo della Carovana (1562), designed by Vasari, with its painted facade, presently housing the main building of the Scuola Normale Superiore di Pisa we pass also the Palazzo dell'Orologio, and the church of S. Stefano dei Cavalieri.

We are now in the center of Pisa and may wander through its ancient streets, lined with beautiful buildings.

San Michele in Borgo

San Michele in Borgo

We will pass the handsome church of S. Michele in Borgo, with Gothic arches and a facade in the Pisan style (14th century).

The church, together with monastery (which first belonged to the Benedictines, and, from the 12th century, the Camaldolese) was built in the late 10th to early 11th century outside the walls of the city, over an ancient temple dedicated to Mars. Both were restored several times in the following ages.

The façade is from the 14th century. The upper part has three order of typically Pisane Gothic loggias. There are three portals, also in Gothic style and with lunettes; the main one is surmounted by a tabernacle with "Madonna and Child" by Lupo di Francesco (the original is in the National Museum of San Matteo in Pisa).

The solemn interior, with a nave and two aisles, houses a *Crucifix* attributed to Nino Pisano (14th century), paintings by Matteo Rosselli, Baccio Lomi, Aurelio Lomi and Giuseppe Melani, as well as remains of frescoes from the 13th century. Under the pavement is the crypt, probably what remains of a former church.

We are then on our way to Piazza Garibaldi, the bustling center of today's city life.

Where to eat in Pisa.

Restaurants in Pisa:

- L'Ostellino Piazza Cavallotti 1, Really great for a fast sandwich, Italian style! Try the Lardo with walnuts and honey! It is possible to get a seat but often the place fills up. Great atmosphere, price and selection spot on!
- Gusto Giusto Via San Giuseppe Cottolengo, 25, +39 340 738 0544 If you have some time at Pisa station and want food it's less than 5 min walk (well worth it). Calling it a 'fast-food' is a dishonor.
- Gusto al 129 - Pizzeria Via Santa Bibbiana, 10, +39 050 620 3117 Great pizza and service from here. It won't hurt if you book in advance. Anyway, the place is small in a good way, the staff is friendly and English speaking, the pizzas are just awesome, full of flavor and you can even watch how your pizza is being made. Prices are average in the city, definitely fair and cheap for what you get.
- Anatolia Kebap da Hasan Via G. Carducci 49, +39 050 520 0872 This little kebab shop/pizzeria sits just off the main thoroughfare between the train station and the leaning tour of Pisa. The staff is cheerful and friendly and provids quick service. The food itself is that of a slightly above average kebab shop with relatively low prices providing good value for money, which given the normal fare and prices in the restaurants surrounding most tourist hot spots is a nice surprise.
- La Curva Via Livornese, 233, +39 050 532 405 The place is rather small, 10 tables at most. The owners are true Sicilian people, despite "taking their time" to serving you, they are very welcoming and gentle and the manager/chef is very passionate about the plates he prepares and it's a pleasure to listen to him explaining them. A tip, don't look at the menu, ask him what's recommended on that day, go for fish, it's marvelous.
- Peperosa Via Renato Fucini 10, +39 050 314 4170 The restaurant is smalll and you need reservation but it deserves

it. Food is pretty good and they have a pretty good and tipical menu. This is not the spot to go to if you are an uncomfortable traveler! This is the place to go to soak up local charm and dine on real home cooking in a city that is overrun by folks who want to see the tower lean. I you have seen the tower and want to experience real Pisan food, try this!

- La Taverna di Pulcinella Via Garofani 10, +39 050 520 2704 Might not be a fancy pizzeria, but the cook makes the simple-yet-delicious pizzas right in front of us. Fresh ingredients, great dough and generously huge portions make for a cheap and delicious meal. Its location is a little hidden - parallel to the main Corso Italia, near the river - but well worth the effort of finding it. They speak little english, but you'll get by. Just eat!
- La taverna di Emma Via Carlo Cammeo, 50, +39 050 555 003 Hard to locate as the name is on the awning. The restaurant itself is stunning, and perfect for romantic meals. Starters are amazing: well decorated, tasty and absolutely massive. If you are not really hungry you better share one in two to save room for the rest. Portions are generally big and full of flavour. Good selection of wines (of course). The service is very friendly and you feel like at home. The place is not big. Few tables available and only indoor. Make an advance booking. The place is getting very popular.
- Lunasia Green Park Resort Via dei Tulipani, 1, +39 050 313 5711 First of all, this place is more than a restaurant. It is a place where they have transformed food to art. The different menus together with excellent service explain why they are awarded with a Michelin star. I can strongly recommend a visit if you want a lifetime experience to a decent price compared to this extremely high level.
- Namaste India Ristorante Via S Benardo 34, +39 050 40 604 The place is always busy or fully booked. The staff are so so friendly and kind, you even receive a rose at the end of your meal for the ladies. The food is really great. The portions are not too big but filling enough. Food is full of flavour and well presented and can not fault at all. So if your in around Pisa

and fancy a change from pizza or pasta, try this Indian restaurant!

- Osteria in domo Via Santa Maria 129, +39 050 555 542 It is a strange place: in a very touristic zone, there is this particular place. Few options, but all extremely good. You would not expect such a quality food place near one of the most famous Italian tourist attractions. Great place to go to enjoy high quality food for a fair price!
- Osteria San Paolo Via San Paolo, 16, +39 050 501194 A nice atmosphere to this restaurant, a bit mixed in terms of decor, mixing modern and old. The menu gives lots of choice. The food is nice and you could tell it is freshly prepared. Off the beaten track quite close to the train station, seems to be popular with the locals. Has mixed starters - with at twist, not the usual cold cuts. Friendly and welcoming staff.

Arriving at Pisa by air.

The airport most used by all of Europe for Tuscany is Pisa's "Galileo Galilei" (PSA), where almost all the "low cost" flights arrive. There's a shuttle service that brings you to Florence in 70 minutes. Be careful however: traffic can be truly intense on the motorway between Florence and Pisa thus creating the possibility of being late and missing your flight! Probably the best solution is to reach Florence by train, using the airport station.

Pisa's is the main airport in Tuscany, with many destinations. It is a focus city of Air One and Ryanair. Delta flies a direct fly from New York's JFK 4 days a week.

By Train-PisaMover Bus

The airport is located just 1 kilometer from the Pisa Central Railway Station. Florence is 1 hour 20 minutes away.

By the end of December 2015 the new fast and fully automatic connection PisaMover will link Pisa Airport to Pisa Central Station in 5/8 minutes every day, from 6 a.m. to 24.00 p.m.

Until the end of 2015 Pisa Airport- Pisa Central Station transfer will be provided by the PisaMover Bus service with a timetable departure of every 10 minutes and a journey time of just 8 minutes.

The Author

Enrico Massetti was born in Milano. Now he lives in Washington DC, USA, but he regularly visits his hometown, and enjoys going around all the places near his home town that can be reached by public transportation.

Enrico can be reached at **enricomassetti@msn.com**.

Photo Credits

Cover - Cathedral and Leaning Tower - Photo © Rodrigo Soldon

Cathedral and Leaning Tower - Photo © Rodrigo Soldon

The Leaning Tower - Photo © Saro di Bartolo

The Baptistery - Photo © Sergio Leenen

Cathedral from the Camposanto - Photo © Ricardo Samaniego

The Duomo - Photos © Visit Tuscany

The Leaning Tower - Photos © McPig

San Paolo a Ripa d'Arno - Photo I Sailko

National Museum of Pisa - Photo in public domain

Palazzo della Carovana - Photo in public domain

San Michele in Borgo - Photo in public domain

Other tourist guides

One day outings from Milan without a car

One day Outings from Milan without a car

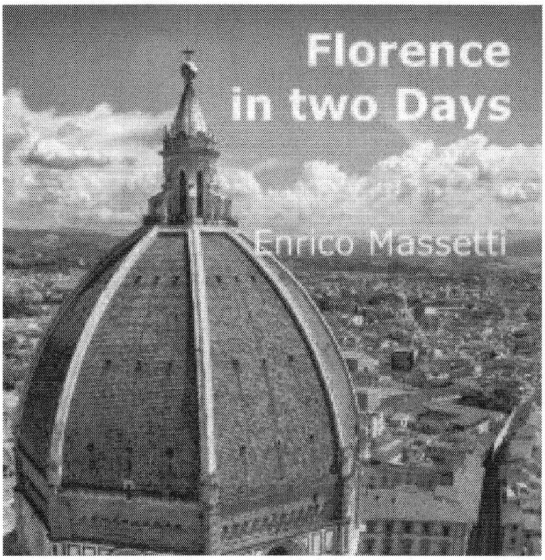

Florence in two days

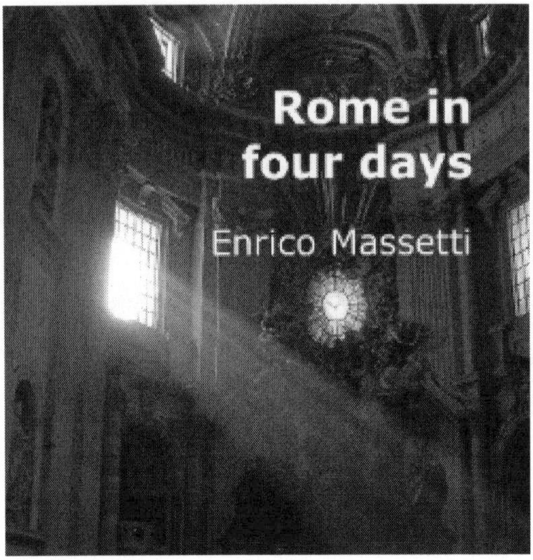

Rome in four days

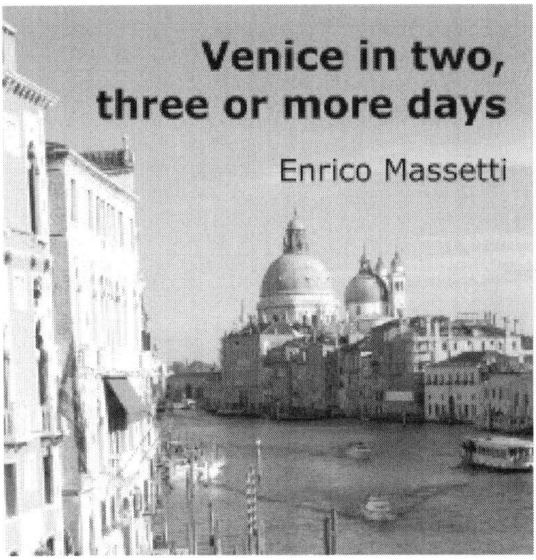

Venice in two days

Table of Contents

Pisa in One Day 1

Pisa 3

The Baptistery 6
The Camposanto 7
The Duomo 8
The Bell Tower known as The Leaning Tower 9
San Paolo a Ripa d'Arno 11
National Museum of Pisa 13
Palazzo della Carovana 14
San Michele in Borgo 15
Where to eat in Pisa 17

Arriving at Pisa by air 20

The Author 21

Photo Credits 22

Other tourist guides 23

11468351R00016

Printed in Great Britain
by Amazon.co.uk, Ltd.,
Marston Gate.